KIDDING AROUND

SEATTLE

A YOUNG PERSON'S GUIDE TO THE CITY

RICK STEVES

ILLUSTRATED BY MELISSA MEIER

John Muir Publications
Santa Fe, New Mexico

For my wife, Anne, and our kids, Andy and Jackie.

Also for my pals: Nick, Stephanie, and Michael; Matthew and Andrew; Alex, Max and Sijai— with big hugs from "Meem."

John Muir Publications, P.O. Box 613, Santa Fe, NM 87504

First edition. Second printing September 1992

Library of Congress Cataloging-in-Publication Data
Steves, Rick, 1955-
    Kidding around Seattle : a young person's guide to the city / Rick Steves; illustrated by Melissa Meier.
        p. cm.
    Includes index.
    Summary: A guide to the geography, history, people, and interesting sites of this northwestern city.
    ISBN 0-945465-84-X
    1. Seattle (Wash.)—Description—Guide-books— Juvenile literature. 2. Children—Travel—Washington— Seattle—Guide-books—Juvenile literature. [1. Seattle (Wash.)—Description—Guides.] I. Meier, Melissa, ill. II. Title.
F899.S43S74 1991
917.97'7720443—dc20   90-27010
                                                          CIP
                                                           AC

Typeface: Trump Mediaeval
Designer: Joanna V. Hill
Typesetter: Copygraphics, Inc., Santa Fe, New Mexico
Printer: Guynes Printing Company of New Mexico

Distributed to the book trade by
W. W. Norton & Company, Inc.
New York, New York

Distributed to the education market by
The Wright Group
19201 120th Avenue N.E.
Bothell, WA 98011-9512

Contents

Packing Tips—*Plan on a few rainy days. Bring a hooded raincoat. Tennis shoes are good for running around in, but a pair of puddle-stompers will come in handy. You'll be making some new friends, so bring a string of postcards or a picture book from your hometown or state for a little travelers' show 'n' tell. Pack a trip diary or journal to fill with all your new ideas, memories, and rain jokes. Bring a belt pouch or backpack so you can stash your souvenirs, pack a picnic, and store your raincoat if the sun comes out.*

Even little squirts like me, Belinda Bivalve, LOVE SEATTLE!!

3

1. Seattle in Your Pocket

S eattle, here you come! If you like puddle stomping, tree climbing, and squirting clams, you'll love Seattle. And even if you're not a clam fan, wet, green, and hilly Seattle is a one-of-a-kind city. It's number one in the U.S.A. in the purchase of windshield wipers, pleasure boats, books (what else to do on a rainy day), and sunglasses (so rarely used, they always get lost).

They say you can tell people who were born in Seattle by their webbed feet. If you see any bare feet during your visit, check them out. But, not counting ducks, you won't find many webbed ones, because the city is such a cool place to live that people from all over have moved here.

The drizzly gray weather is just about the only bad thing about Seattle. But the major worry here is drowning in new neighbors, not rainfall. Local people use rain scare tactics to keep out-of-towners from moving in. So when you go home, tell your friends that people in Seattle don't tan, they rust.

Seattle-ites are wild about the wilderness. Their world is a natural playground of seashores, lakes, and green mountains. One out of six people owns a boat. More people live on houseboats than anywhere this side of Asia. Lots of people

Seattle, with half a million people, is not huge. You could fit everybody in the city into seven big football stadiums. Or 10,000 school buses. It's the 25th biggest city in the U.S.A., about the size of Denver. Another million people live in Seattle's suburbs. Most of them work and play in Seattle and call themselves Seattle-ites.

4

drive an hour or so after work for a little night skiing at several nearby ski resorts. Lakes, beaches, remote islands, bike trails, national forests, and mountain escapes make even grown-ups play hooky sometimes.

Seattle is a fun mix of pioneer history, old-time markets, Indian stories, chummy seagulls, a world-class zoo, exotic food, speedy elevators, Gold Rush rowdiness, an aquarium that friendly fish love to call home, and soggy people.

Study this book. It's your step-by-step handbook for the best kidding-around time any Seattle visitor ever had. Don't worry, I promise there will be no test. But if you really use all the ideas in your *Kidding Around Seattle* book, you'll have way more fun than staying home. And don't forget to bring your parents. Seattle's a place even Mom and Dad can kid around in.

The Seattle Rain Festival is held from August 1 through July 31, every year. Seattle gets more hours of rain than almost anyplace. Decent places like Houston, New York, and Washington, D.C., get more inches of rain, but Seattle really savors each gallon, letting it dribble down in a slow grey drizzle. Seattle gets about a week of snow a year and is almost never really hot or cold.

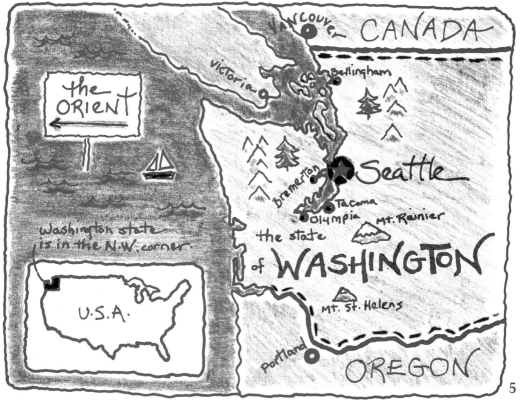

2. The Seattle Story

Seattle was named after a very wise, friendly, and peaceful Indian chief. According to an Indian legend, when someone says your name after you die, you spin around in your grave. Pioneers were just trying to be nice to Chief Seattle. But if the legend's true, the chief is probably pretty dizzy by now. By the way, his real name was Sealth, but the pioneers changed it to Seattle for easier pronounciation.

ou've climbed trees older than Seattle. If our fifty states were a family, Washington would be one of the youngest kids. Back when Abe Lincoln was young, only Indians lived here—in split cedar wood "long houses." When they went hunting in the summer, they slept in "tents" of light woven mats. They respected and loved the land. Today's Washingtonians are an echo of the Indians who lived here before them. They live in wooden houses, love to go tenting in the summer, and are famous for their love of nature.

In the 1700s, explorers from Spain, Russia, France, and a brand-new little country called the United States sailed in and out of the area's bays and harbors looking mostly for animal furs and the elusive "Northwest Passage." Everybody dreamed about the Northwest Passage, an ice-free shortcut that would let them sail from the Atlantic to the Pacific without having to go all the way around South America.

California and Oregon were already states when the first settlers came to Seattle. In 1851, nine parents with twelve kids set up camp on Alki Point (today's West Seattle). A few wet and hungry years later, Henry Yesler brought in a steam-powered sawmill and Seattle had some business: sawing lumber for the growing cities of California.

Trees were toppled, and the logs were skidded down "skid road" (today's Yesler Way) to the sawmill on the harbor. From 1850 to 1870, the logging town grew up around Pioneer Square and Yesler Way.

Most of the local Indians were very friendly. There was one tiny war. Only two pioneers were killed, but lots of people who had planned to move here were scared out of the idea when they heard the story.

Boom Town Burns Down

Seattle boomed in the 1880s. The railroad came to town, and lots of little ferryboats connected it with towns around the Puget Sound. Sawing lumber for the rebuilding of San Francisco (which had recently burned down), mining coal for heat, and growing hops (the plant used for making beer) all gave Seattle lots of jobs, lots of money, and too many beer bellies. Locals said you could smell Seattle a mile or two before you could see it. In only ten years Seattle grew from 3,500 people to 42,000 people. It grew recklessly into some big problems.

When the center of Seattle shifted and logging died down, Seattle's "Skid Road" became the hangout of down-and-out people, the homeless, and panhandlers. This was the original "Skid Row," and now the hard-luck streets of cities all over the U.S.A. are called "skid rows."

In 1897, about 100,000 people headed north for the gold rush; 30,000 got there, 300 got rich, and 50 stayed rich. Very bad odds.

8

Cluttered, congested, crazy Seattle was a fire just waiting to happen. And happen it did—in 1889, in the middle of the city. Water pressure was lousy, the fire chief was out of town, everything was hot and dry, and a strong wind blew the flames right into 50 tons of ammunition. The little fire became a giant fire. It was so big that the city fire-fighters just ran for the hills and watched. Sloppy Seattle burned down.

Gold, Airplanes, and Modern Seattle

Determined to make the fire a blessing in disguise, the people rebuilt their city better than ever. They leveled hills, filled in mud flats, built elevated streets, and made buildings out of fireproof bricks. Seattle was "new and improved." Even the toilets worked. The buildings you see today around Pioneer Square were built during this construction wave. In 1892, they were the best and fanciest buildings west of Chicago.

Seattle was ready when the 1897 Klondike gold rush hit. Masses of prospectors, feverish with get-rich-quick dreams, came to Seattle on their way to faraway gold fields in Canada and Alaska. Though a few prospectors got rich, the real winner was Seattle, which fed, clothed, and entertained those crazy gold miners.

Much of early Seattle was built on stilts along a mucky shore. Some people could flush their toilets only at low tides. Some very high tides turned unlucky toilets into totally gross fountains. Well-thumbed tide charts hung in many bathrooms. Some streets, even, were built on stilts. Once a boy fell off a street corner and drowned.

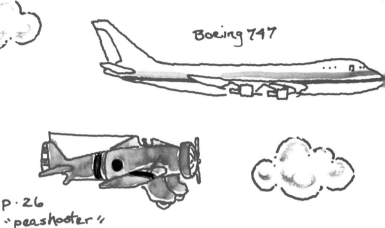

Boeing 747

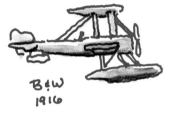

B&W 1916

p. 26 "peashooter"

Young and growing Seattle needed people, especially women. A clever guy named Asa Mercer went to New England around 1865 to take care of this shortage. Here come the brides! Asa brought back 57 young women. Many were ladies whose husbands were killed in the Civil War who wanted new husbands. Asa became very popular, a local hero even. These "Mercer Girls" were classy. They brought culture and education to rough and rowdy Seattle. Today, many of Seattle's most influential families are their great-great-grandchildren.

Seattle was becoming one rude city, the gateway to gold, Alaska, and the Orient. In 1909, a huge party, the Alaska-Yukon-Pacific Exhibition, was held so everyone around the country could see how important Seattle was. It was one excellent party. Nearly four million people came. The party grounds became the impressive University of Washington campus (which today keeps about 30,000 students busy studying and learning).

To make matters even better, in 1916 a man named Boeing launched his first "float plane" to fly the first loads of airmail to Canada. The First World War needed lots of planes, and the Boeing Airplane Company was on its way to the business big time. Soon it was Seattle's top source of jobs. People from as far away as Oshkosh and Orlando came, excited about making $5 a day. Today a Boeing worker earns that much in 15 minutes, and Boeing is Seattle's top employer and the world's top source of commercial airplanes.

In 1962, Seattle put together its second successful mega-party, the "Century 21" World's

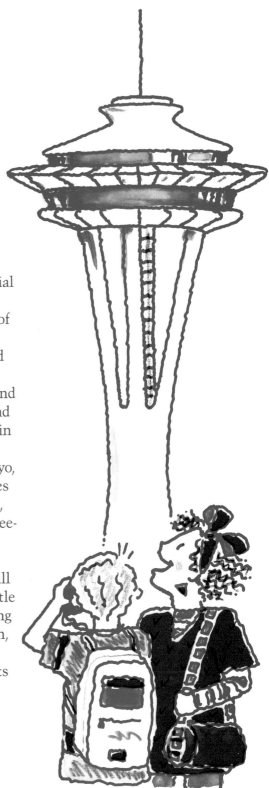

Fair. This boosted Seattle from a nothing-special kind of place to an almost glamorous city attracting businesses, movie makers, and lots of people like you—tourists. The leftovers of the world's fair, among them the Space Needle and the Science Center, are today's Seattle Center, the place where visitors and locals go for fun and food, rock and Bach, rides and rallies, hoops and hockey. If there had been no 1962 World's Fair in Seattle, maybe you wouldn't even be visiting.

Seattle's economy is like a slow-moving yo-yo, and Boeing holds the string. When Boeing takes a business nosedive, so does Seattle. One time, so many people left that a big sign above the freeway said, "Will the last person to leave Seattle please turn out the lights?"

But things are better now. The 1990 Goodwill Games directed the national spotlight on Seattle again. Today the "Emerald City" is busy fighting the normal big city problems such as pollution, traffic jams, crime, drugs, homelessness, and overdevelopment. Seattle works hard to earn its title as the "most livable" city in the United States.

3. Pioneer Square

Totem poles are tall wooden statues carved by Northwest Indians to tell the history of their tribe. The bears and eagles and raccoons represent their distant grandparents.

On Pioneer "Square" (actually a triangle), you get the very best feel for the Seattle of a hundred years ago, pioneers' Seattle. The fancy old glass and iron thing in the square is called the **Pergola**. People used to wait here for the trolleys back when your grandparents were in diapers. The street lights are just as old.

Find the **totem pole**, a reminder of Seattle's Indian roots. Have a drink of water at the Chief Seattle (Sealth) statue. Look into the chief's bronze eyes. Does he look as wise and friendly as everyone says he was?

You are surrounded by the buildings of the new and improved Seattle of 1889, built after that terrible fire. The **Merchant's Cafe** is the city's oldest restaurant. A stairway leads down to a whole dusty pile of antique shops. Many shops have a free guidebook full of more information on Seattle's most historic square. Look to the west; the waterfront is just a slip and a somersault away.

For the goofiest historic walk in the world, go underground. Every hour a gaggle of curious visitors follow a funny guide from Doc Maynard's Restaurant into a goofy ghost town called **Underground Seattle**. You'll walk hidden sidewalks

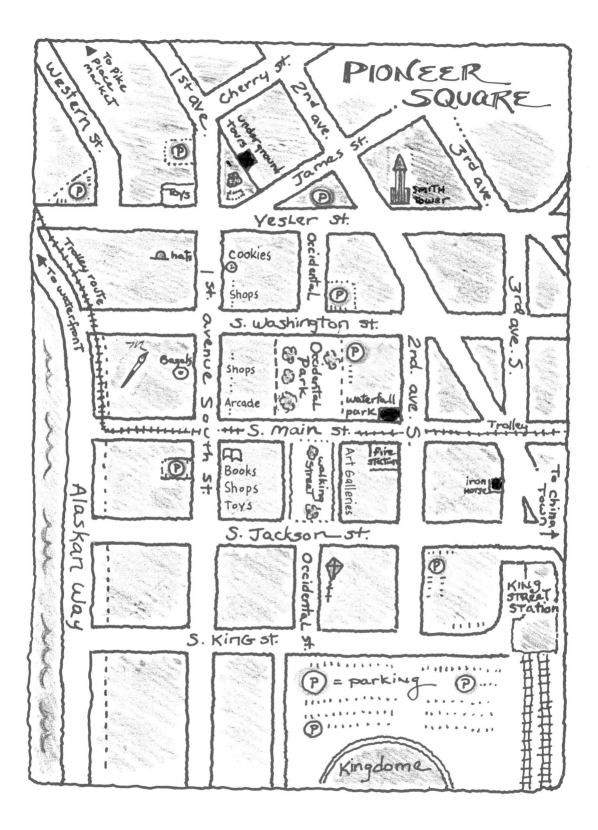

Pioneer Square is Seattle's "home" for the homeless. When people have to live in the streets, sometimes they get so dirty and dangerous-looking that you almost forget that they are people just like you and your friends. Many of them got kicked out of their homes or apartments when they lost their jobs, many are sick or have alcohol problems. Some live on handouts from passersby and sleep on the benches here, in nearby alleys, or in the nearby homeless shelters. Why do you think such a rich and lucky country as ours has more than three million homeless people?

right out of the 1890s. The ninety-minute tours make history as fun as jumping in jello.

The **Smith Tower** was a big deal when it was built in 1914. In fact, for 25 years it was the biggest deal west of the Mississippi. And even though today we think it's a quaint memory of the old days, the 42-story tower was the tallest building in Seattle until 1969! Walk under angry-looking Indians on the ceiling of the lobby and ride the cool elevators to the great view from the 35th floor. They just don't make elevators like this anymore, complete with shiny, fancy copper decorations and still operated by an attendant—very rare these days.

Watch the lawyers' offices as you rocket smoothly up to the **Chinese Room**, filled with carved teak wood that came all the way from China. The Empress of China donated the fancy Queen's chair. (Be careful: they say any girl who sits in it will be married within one year.) Stroll around the catwalk. What a view! Look down at the buildings of 1889, then flip over to the new skyscrapers. Now that's growth. Trace the waterfront. How many places can you recognize? Look at all the blue and red containers and those giant cranes. That's how a big city like Seattle stays in business. To get the elevator operator to return, push the button. Look down the shaft as the elevator rises to pick you up.

a view of the Smith Tower

In Pioneer Square you'll find...

cookies & croissants

Toys

Hats

wind Socks

All kinds of ART

The **Klondike Gold Rush Museum** calls itself a national park. (Can you imagine a national park inside a building?) Drop in. It's free, and there are lots of exhibits and old movies. Friendly rangers can actually demonstrate old-fashioned gold panning if you ask.

Speaking of parks, head on up to 2nd and South Main to see brick-paved **Occidental Square**. Half a block away is a breezy waterfall garden park with picnic tables hiding in the shadow of all these skyscrapers and cars. If you like fire engines, there's a bunch of them complete with friendly fire-fighters just across the street.

Pioneer Square has some interesting shops. The **Wood Shop** is cracking with fun wooden and furry toys. The **Elliott Bay Bookshop** has enough books in its kids' section to sink a library. The classy cafe downstairs is a good place to store your parents for a while. At **Glass House Art Glass** you can watch experts make and blow glass. This place is hot, 2,000 degrees hot. The **Magic Mouse** squeals with two floors of teddies, puzzles, games, and books. **Ruby Montana's** store full of tacky, wacky gadgets is at 2nd and James. Need a private eye? There's one advertised in the second-story window at 1st and Yesler. Also nearby are a fun hat shop called **We Hats** and a breezy kite shop.

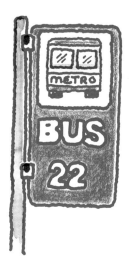

City bus rides are free in the whole downtown area of Seattle. Seattle's helpful "Metro" public transportation system was voted best in the country by the American Public Transit Association. The waterfront trolley and the monorail from downtown to the Seattle Center make getting around part of the fun. For bus, trolley, and monorail information, call 447-4800.

The Kingdome was the site of the biggest holiday party ever—103,000 people (in two sittings) came to the Boeing Corporation's annual Christmas party here. (Guess what they used for "missile" toe?)

Seattle's domed stadium, called the **Kingdome**, is extremely big—as tall as a 25-story building and 660 feet across. If you laid the Space Needle down inside, you could spin it around and around and it would never touch the walls!

This giant, concrete, mushroomlike stadium lets as many as 70,000 screaming fans enjoy football, baseball, motorcycle racing, and rock 'n' roll out of the rain. The giant TV screen is bigger than your living room! The Kingdome claims to have the world's biggest self-supporting concrete roof. If you'd like to roam Seattle's dome, catch the tour for a one-hour behind-the-scenes look at the giant interior, press box, locker rooms (notice how the basketball players have 8-foot-tall shower nozzles), and sports museum.

16

4. The International District

If you lived with your friends in China, the Chinese would call your neighborhood "Yankee Town" and they'd bring their children to take pictures of you in your fluorescent windbreaker and hightops. They'd go to Yankee restaurants to eat funny foreign specialties like hamburgers and french fries and suck on gross milkshakes. When you visit Seattle's International District, it's kind of like that—just in reverse!

little chunk of Asia is just a few blocks from Pioneer Square. Seattle's "Chinatown" is filled with real neighborhoods from almost every part of Asia. The people who live here are normal families from far away, and because they are from far away, they eat and dress and play in some special ways.

Seattle's Chinatown has a sad history. Way back in the 1800s, lots of Chinese people worked to help build the great railroad network that ties our country together. They also labored to rebuild Seattle after the great fire. But when there was no great need for cheap workers, the white workers didn't like the Chinese because they worked for less money. Riots and tension filled the streets, and sometimes the Asians were chased out of town. Life was hard. A popular saying among whites was, "He doesn't have a Chinaman's chance," which means he'll certainly lose or fail.

In World War II, after Japan bombed Pearl Harbor, many innocent Japanese Americans were put into special prison camps and they lost everything. The big freeway nearby (you can hear

its traffic roar) covers land that used to be Japanese homes. Today, many of Seattle's most respected families live in this neighborhood. They welcome you to drop in for a visit.

An Asian Cultural Scavenger Hunt
To explore the International District, walk up King Street to the freeway and down Jackson Street. You can see an herbalist (a shop that sells natural herbs for medicine), a bakery filled with 25-cent ways to send your taste buds to China, extraterrestrial grocery stores, barbecued ducks looking sad and spicy in windows, Kung Fu shops, a fortune cookie factory, and lots more. As long as the telephone booths look like pagodas, you're still in Chinatown.

For your best look at the district and its fascinating history, visit the **Wing Luke Museum**. This cozy little museum lets you do some weaving, learn about silk making and herbal medicine, and see how the early Asian Seattleites lived. It has a fun dimestore-type gift shop.

Visit **Uwajimaya**, the largest Japanese store in the United States. Buy some *oishie* (delicious) munchies you've never thought of eating before. How about seaweed (nori) or tiny dried fish (spit out the eyeballs) on aisles 8 and 9? Find your own UFO (unidentifiable food object). Cruise over to the fish corner to check out the tub of gross old geoducks (pronounced "gooey ducks"). Look at those huge, fat tongues hanging out. (I hope they're tongues!) You'll see crabs as crowded as sardines, plus clams, mussels, and oysters.

Upstairs from the geoducks is the very Japanese gift shop with Japanese teen mags, a fun little $1 childrens' guide to origami, and Asian

books. Look at a book. They are read back to front instead of front to back—completely backwards!

The old trolley rattles visitors from the International District to the Seattle waterfront every half hour.

Let's Eat!

For lots of exotic nibbles that roll to you on a tasty trolley, have a Chinese smorgasbord called dim sum. **King Cafe** is noisy and most authentic. **House of Hong** is big and less exotic but more popular, with lots of trolley action. Both are dim sum yummy. If you're in a noodle mood go to **Ocean City Restaurant**. It should be named Noodle City, swarming with locals, fun and colorful.

Back down toward the Kingdome, for something very American, grab lunch at the **Iron Horse Restaurant**. If you like trains, you'll love this place. Your hamburger and fries are delivered to your table by a tiny electric locomotive. Now that's service! Chew-chew!

5. Ferryboats, Clams, and Sea Gulls—The Waterfront

In the old days, the local Duwamish Indians called the Elliott Bay waterfront "Little Crossing Place." That's **Djidjila'letch** *in the Duwamish language.*

Can you say that 10 times really fast?

Seattle's waterfront is one long, skinny party. Between the major league harbor with its mountains of containerized cargo and giant orange cranes at one end and the grassy park of kites, roller skaters, and joggers at the other end are a mile and a half of reasons to stay out in the rain.

Spend an afternoon pretending it's recess and this waterfront is your salty playground. The fun stretches from Pier 52 (south) to Pier 70 (north). It used to be no fun, just eighteen docks of big freighters and passenger ships coming and going. The business was business. Today the business is fun—fun restaurants, fat seagulls, slap-happy boat rides, and weird shops, all connected by an old-fashioned trolley.

The south end is the heavy-duty work area with the big man-made Harbor Island and lots of cranes. There's good viewing of all the container loading from the periscopes at **Pier 48**. From the nearby **Ferry Terminal**, at Pier 52, you can take a ride on a ferry (that's "ferry'"—not like Tinkerbell) to Bainbridge Island for a watery look at Puget Sound and an eye-popping view of Seattle. It's cheap and boats leave every 30 minutes. Next door, or I should say, next dock, are the fire boats

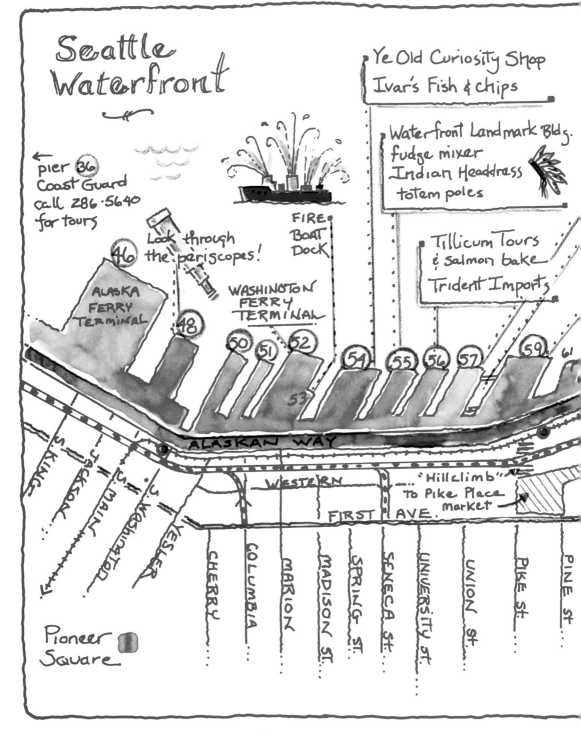

Seattle Waterfront

Ye Old Curiosity Shop
Ivar's Fish & chips

Waterfront Landmark Bldg.
fudge mixer
Indian Headdress
totem poles

← pier 36
Coast Guard
call 286·5640
for tours

Tillicum Tours
& Salmon bake
Trident Imports

Look through
the periscopes!

FIRE
BOAT
Dock

46

ALASKA
FERRY
TERMINAL

48

WASHINGTON
FERRY
TERMINAL

50 51 52

53

54 55 56 57 59 61

ALASKAN WAY

WESTERN

"Hillclimb"
To Pike Place
market

FIRST   AVE.

S. KING
S. JACKSON
S. MAIN
S. WASHINGTON
YESLER

CHERRY
COLUMBIA
MARION
MADISON ST.
SPRING ST.
SENECA ST.
UNIVERSITY ST.
UNION ST.
PIKE St.
PINE St.

Pioneer
Square

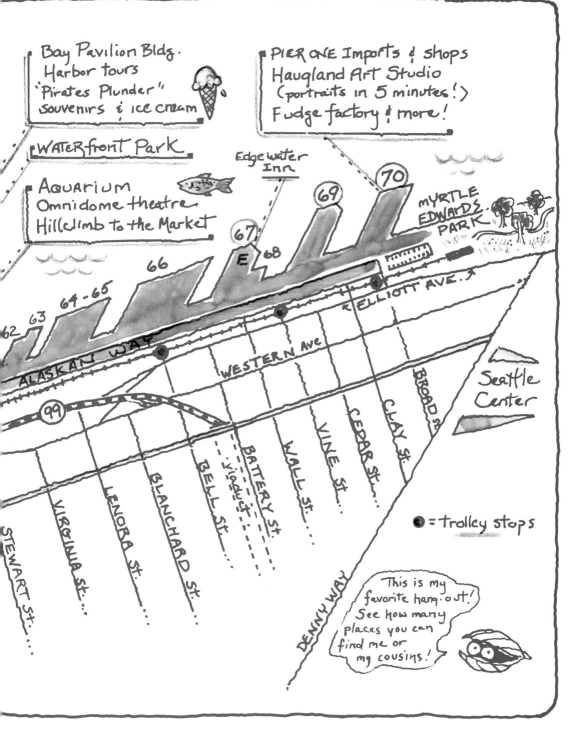

Bay Pavilion Bldg.
Harbor tours
"Pirates Plunder"
souvenirs & ice cream

PIER ONE Imports & shops
Haugland Art Studio
(portraits in 5 minutes!)
Fudge factory & more!

WATERfront Park

Edgewater Inn

AQUARIUM
Omnidome theatre
Hillclimb to the Market

MYRTLE EDWARDS PARK

70

69

67

E   68

66

64-65

63

62

ELLIOTT AVE.

ALASKAN WAY

WESTERN AVE.

BROAD St.

CLAY St.

CEDAR St.

VINE St.

WALL St.

BATTERY St. viaduct

BELL St.

BLANCHARD St.

LENORA St.

VIRGINIA St.

STEWART St.

DENNY WAY

99

Seattle Center

● = trolley stops

This is my favorite hang-out! See how many places you can find me or my cousins!

Ride the trolley. It's from Australia. If it was a person it could retire now, but this 65-year-old vehicle keeps working. It costs 60 cents (exact change only), and you can get on and off wherever you like for 90 minutes.

Seattle Funplex—1541 15th West, 285-7842 (a mile north of the piers): Deluxe 19-hole mini-golf course, Seattle's only indoor laser tag arena, a batting cage (grab a bat, put on a helmet and get ready for a fast ball), slot cars, more video and sports games than any place in Seattle, a people maze, snack bar with pizzas, and a small kids play area. Open daily from 11 a.m. until way past your bedtime. It's great fun, but get ready to bust your budget.

and an old fire truck (open 1:00-5:00 p.m. and 7:00-9:00 p.m., free tours, just drop in). Once a week, the boats sail and test their spouts.

Since 1899, **Ye Olde Curiosity Shoppe** at Pier 54 has entertained its shoppers with a fascinating pile of mummies, a snail as heavy as you, fake barf, joke postcards, and souvenirs. It's a fun place. **Pier 57** is a waterfront park, with fishing, ice cream, two-hour harbor tours, and fine views.

The highlight of the waterfront is the **Pier 59 Aquarium**. Fish love Seattle's aquarium. All the slimy, scaly, big-eyed creatures of Puget Sound bubble their days away in fancy tanks. The aquarium has a touch tank, a giant underwater dome, a busy salmon ladder, and enough marine otters, seals, and octopi for everybody. Don't miss the sharks in the Pacific Coral Reef, the coconut-cracking, tree-climbing crustaceans (land crabs), and the seal meals (feeding times are 11:30, 2:00, and 5:00). A lot of Seattle people get married under the water dome. The fish love it.

The **Omnidome** theater is just a clam squirt away. This is a giant curved screen theater that shows ultra-real nature movies. Plop down on the most comfortable seat a tired tourist like you ever plopped down on (the ones in the front have the best view for people who don't get seasick) and wrap yourself up in film. Every half hour the eruption of Mt. Saint Helens blazes on screen (you swoop by helicopter right into the crater), followed by a second "nature on loud" feature.

Across the street is the hill-climb to the Pike Place Market (see chapter 6). Wimps can ride the elevator.

Let's Eat!

The **Old Spaghetti Factory** (opposite Pier 70) is cheap and fun. Every spaghetti meal comes with any kind of sauce you want, hot bread, and cold ice cream. Ask to be seated in the 1917 train car or even in a big bed!

Ivar's Acres of Clams and Fish Bar at Pier 54 has a fun feed-the-seagulls outdoor setting or heated shelter on the waterfront with great takeout fish, clams, clam nectar, and views. The atmosphere is as salty as your fries. Inside, the classier restaurant offers a perfect Seattle dinner as the sun melts over the Olympics and the ferries slice across Puget Sound. The lobby is a museum of dugout canoes and old Seattle photos. The **Pier 70 Restaurant and Chowder House** has fresh seafood, colorable menus, and goofy drinks.

For a combination cruise, fascinating harbor tour, Indian dance, salmon baked the traditional Indian way, and a chance to visit an island state park, catch the boat that cruises from Pier 56 to **Tillicum Village** *on Blake Island. Eat steamed clams on the beach, feed friendly deer, and watch Indian dancers wearing 6-foot masks with huge wooden beaks slamming open and shut while you eat your buffet dinner.*

6. From the Pike Place Market to the Skyscrapers

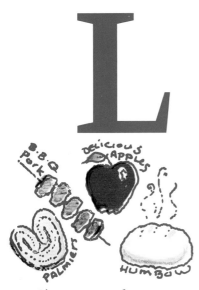

If it's a sunny day, get a few bucks from your favorite adult and offer to put together the most memorable picnic you'll ever try to forget. Make it a scavenger hunt for new and incredible edibles, and figure out why they're called "food-stuffs."

Look out, screaming fishermen are tossing slippery fish at the **Pike Place Market**. Seattle has the oldest continuously operated farmer's market in the United States.

The market is a trip through the food hall of fame, an edible explosion. Noisy salesmen throw salmon like slimy footballs, handcuffed lobsters are none too happy, clams squirt people who aren't on the lookout, apples shine like light bulbs, very orange oranges are stacked in perfect pyramids, invisible things smell very good, crabs get crabby in beds of ice, Chuck Geoduck is flirting with Belinda Bivalve, and a hundred farmers all think their broccoli and kiwis are in some kind of beauty pageant. The fat and happy master of ceremonies is the well-fed bronze pig who greets you under the most famous and oldest chunk of neon in Seattle, the Pike Place Market sign. Street musicians strum and sing while kids munch and slurp. Notice all the floor tiles with names on them. These people donated money to help save the market.

Wander up and down and around and around. You'll find nooks and crannies full of funky shops cluttered with dusty antiques, tattered

PUBLIC MARKET CENTER

The Pike Place Market started 80 years ago when local moms tossed out the greedy middlemen and demanded the chance to buy their pumpkins straight from the guy who grew them. In the 1970s, the grandkids of those heroic early shoppers saved the market from becoming another condo city. Today it's a registered National Historic Site and the biggest mom-and-pop store in town.

PICKED DAILY

PIKE PLACE MARKET
"✖" marks the FUN map

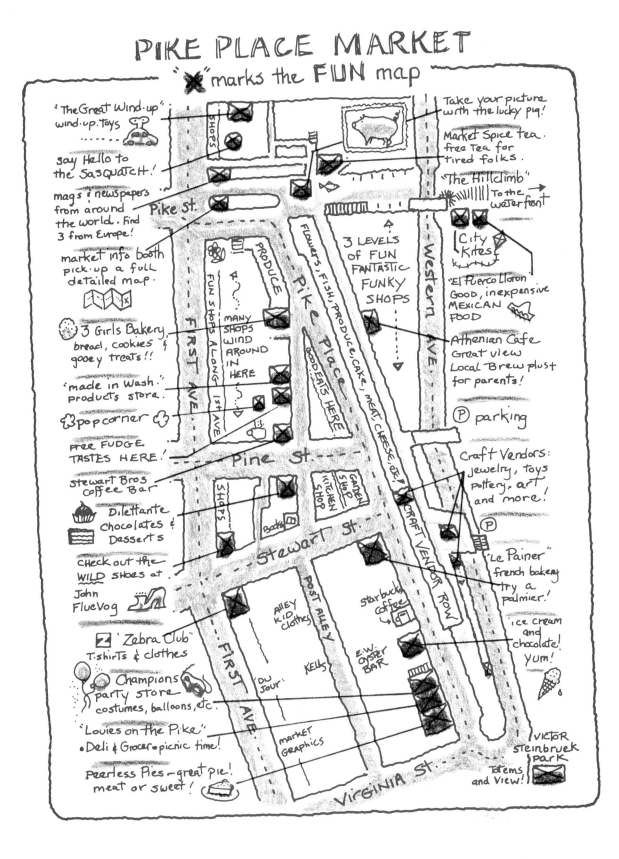

"The Great Wind·up" wind·up toys

Say Hello to the SASQUATCH!

mags & newspapers from around the world. Find 3 from Europe!

Pike St.

market info booth pick·up a full detailed map.

3 Girls Bakery bread, cookies & gooey treats!!

"made in Wash." products store.

pop corner

FREE FUDGE TASTES HERE!

Stewart Bros coffee Bar

Dilettante Chocolates & Desserts

check out the WILD shoes at. John FlueVog

"Zebra Club" T·shirts & clothes

Champions party store costumes, balloons, etc.

"Louies on the Pike" ·Deli & Grocer·picnic time!

Peerless Pies—great pie! meat or sweet!

Take your picture with the lucky pig!

Market Spice tea. free tea for tired folks.

"The Hillclimb" To the waterfront

City Kites

"El Puerco Lloron" Good, inexpensive MEXICAN FOOD

Athenian Cafe Great view Local Brew plus! for parents!

P parking

Craft Vendors: Jewelry, toys Pottery, art and more!

"Le Painer" french bakery try a palmier!

ice cream and chocolate! yum!

VICTOR STEINBRUEK PARK Totems and View!

SHOPS

3 LEVELS of FUN FANTASTIC FUNKY SHOPS

FLOWERS, FISH, PRODUCE, CAKE, MEAT CHEESE, etc!

PRODUCE

Pike Place

FUN SHOPS ALONG 1st AVE.

MANY SHOPS WIND AROUND IN HERE

GOOD EATS HERE

FIRST AVE.

Pine St.

GARDEN SHOP
KITCHEN SHOP

Books

Stewart St.

CRAFT VENDOR ROW

SHOPS

ALLEY KID clothes

POST ALLEY

KELLS

DU JOUR

MARKET GRAPHICS

starbucks coffee

E.W. OYSTER BAR

FIRST AVE.

Western Ave.

P

VIRGINIA St.

comic books, old war medals, baseball cards, and goofy wind-up toys.

Go early any day (except winter Sundays) to see the farmers stack their mushrooms and aim their carrots. This is when the expert shoppers drop by. Weekends are best for artsy craftsy things. For the best time possible, follow this "X Marks the Fun" map.

Seattle's modern business district is a short waddle from the older and wetter parts of downtown. The shiny black **Columbia Center** is the highest skyscraper west of Houston. One of Seattle's most famous free view points is from the rest rooms on the top floor.

The **Freeway Park** and convention and trade center are a smart solution to a city sliced by eight lanes of traffic. They were built over the freeway! Now Seattle enjoys a 5-acre tree-filled park with man-made waterfalls and a convention center within easy walking distance from the top hotels and shops. The convention center is the ultimate high-tech meeting place, with movable walls, speedy escalators, and lots of green glass.

Freeway Park is where local workers go for the adult equivalent of recess. Hear the soothing gurgle of 27,000 gallons of recycled water a minute smothering the sound of the 150,000 cars that zoom by underneath each day. At lunchtime, it often throbs with live music. Ask about summer concerts.

The **Westlake Center**, a spanky new mall right in the middle of downtown, teases you with four floors of shopping. The fast food is on the top floor. Drop into the Disney Store, and giggle at bigger-than-life cartoons that play all day long. Underground passages connect this mall with the Bon Marche, Frederick & Nelson, and Nordstrom's department stores.

Soar from the mall to the Space Needle on the monorail. The station for this elevated one-track

Seattle's three TV stations offer tours and some easy chances to be in the studio audience. All are downtown and need you in their audiences: King (NBC, 448-3795, Seattle Today, a morning interview program, and its popular comedy show, Almost Live), and KOMO (ABC, 443-4000, for its Northwest Afternoon interview show and for its provocative Town Meeting). KIRO (728-7777) offers tours but has no live audiences.

railroad is on the third floor. Or hop an escalator down, down, down to an underground bus station bright with fancy light fixtures and artwork. Electric buses whoosh underfoot, on the level below. Pop back out of the station at Westlake Plaza, where you can sample Seattle's own Cow Chip Cookies and a frothy glass of milk before you dare to walk through water (without getting your sneakers wet!) at the shimmering, freestanding waterfall.

7. Seattle Center

The Seattle Center attracts more kids and families than any amusement park in the United States, except the two Disney places. And it's always hopping with people and activities. There are more than 5,000 events a year—that's about fifteen a day!

When your parents were kids, this place was the ultimate in space age technology: a towering space needle with a slowly spinning restaurant on top, a bubble-ator (a glass ball of an elevator), a sleek monorail, and tons of spacey architecture. Thirty years after its birth, the Seattle Center looks quaint compared to the skyscrapers that have sprung up since. Even if it is a pretty old-fashioned version of the future, the Seattle Center is a great place for a visit, especially for kids.

In 1962, the Russians were flying circles around us in space and the United States needed a kick in the rocket booster. The 1962 World's Fair was in Seattle and the theme was "Century 21." Lucky for Seattle, the fair left the city with a neat new park. Today Seattle enjoys its 74 acres of fountains, concert halls, sports arenas, rides, restaurants, and shopping places.

Seattle's most famous building is the 600-foot-tall **Space Needle**. The fastest elevator you'll ever almost throw up in zips you 520 feet up at ten miles per hour. That takes 41 seconds. The elevator operator gives you the fastest-talking tour you'll ever hear, and the huge elevator windows make you feel like you're hanging onto a spaceship at lift-off.

Best view in Town!

If you see only one thing in Seattle, see everything—from the Space Needle observatory deck. There are telescopes, lots of wind, and tourists from faraway countries, especially Asia. Seattle is the gateway to Japan and the Orient. Inside are plenty of tacky souvenirs in the highest shop in Seattle, as well as video games, snacks, drinks, and an information display where you can learn everything you never wanted to know about the Needle. For example, this thing needs 1,340 gallons of paint for a paint job!

The Space Needle restaurant, powered by a lawn mower-size motor, revolves once every hour. So every table gets an all around great view. Kids get half-price meals and diners get a free elevator ride up. If you leave your bag on the window sill, it'll be back in 60 minutes. While you're waiting for your meal (or your bag), ask your parents what life was like back in 1962 when this place was "Jetson City."

For some good, old-fashioned, smear-cotton-candy-all-over-your-face-and-spin-your-guts-out fun, swing by the **Seattle Center Fun Forest**—you'll see it just under the Space Needle. It's your basic amusement park, with rides, an arcade, and plenty of ways to stay out of trouble.

The **Monorail** (next to the rides) was way ahead of its time in 1962, and in the United States, it still is. This 90-second, 1.2-mile ride is a cheap, easy, and fun way to zip from the Seattle Center to the fancy Westlake Mall in the downtown shopping area. Sit in front next to the driver for the best view. The driver is usually a fun-to-talk-to person who loves to tell people about how great this monorail is. "First one in the U.S.A., it carries the most passengers and is more powerful than any other." Whizzing smoothly along its merry way on an elevated track, the electricity-powered monorail is great in a flood. It runs its little round-trip journey every 15 minutes from 10:00 a.m. until midnight (until 9:00 p.m. weeknights during the off-season). Ride it even if you're going nowhere. Round-trips are fast and fun.

Hey dude! Science isn't a subject. It's an experience! The **Pacific Science Center** brings out the Mr. Science in everybody. It's a hands-on party of touch tanks, huge bubbles, giant screens, and major lasers.

Pick up the map and schedule and plan your visit so you'll get to see everything. You can easily spend three hours here lost in your own space. Ready for an adventure? Work your way, clockwise, around the Science Center.

First, for a great way to really know thyself, start at the Body Works. Are you color blind?

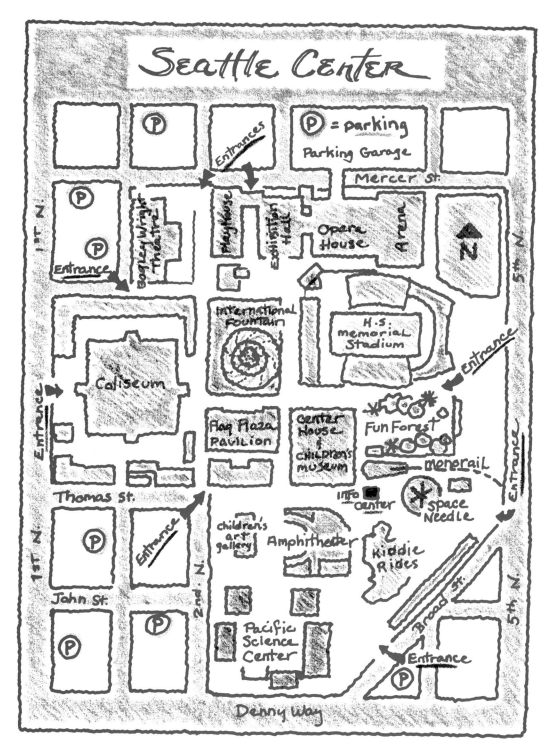

Seattle Center

P = parking
Parking Garage

Entrances

Mercer St.

1st N.

Bagley Wright Theatre

Playhouse

Exhibition Hall

Opera House

Arena

N

5th N.

Entrance

Entrance

International Fountain

Coliseum

H.S. memorial Stadium

Entrance

Fun Forest

Flag Plaza Pavilion

Center House & Children's Museum

monorail

Entrance

info Center

Space Needle

Thomas St.

2nd N.

Entrance

children's art gallery

Amphitheater

Kiddie Rides

John St.

Broad St.

5th N.

Pacific Science Center

Entrance

Denny Way

35

How much pedaling does it take to burn off the calories of one cookie? Now rearrange your face on a TV screen. How does your nose smell? Take a close look at some blood under a microscope. Or just play around on the computers. All this boning up on your body works up an appetite. Upstairs, the **Fountains Cafe** serves sandwiches, soups, and snacks.

The **Science Playground** will tickle your mind. Want to hold a two-day-old chick, pet a sea anemone, shake hands with a starfish, zap your shadow onto a fluorescent wall and make it stick, see a beehive close up, or film yourself playing news reporter on KKID-TV? Also, be sure to check out the **Planetarium**. It's out of this world. (The schedule lists the free showings.)

Just for Tots is for little brothers and sisters who like making big bubbles, scribbling, and squirting things. Moms and dads really appreciate this place.

Now head into the **Sea Monster House**. This is an Indian long house showing just how the original Seattle-ites lived.

Outside is the **physics playground**, your perfect chance to ride a gyroscope, time your echo, and lift 500 pounds (equal to about about how many moms?) all by yourself. . .with a little help from a lever.

Wow, I get exhausted just writing about this fun science stuff. For a chance to sit down and enjoy the wonders of nature and technology on a movie screen taller than a three-story building and wider than a grocery store, see the **IMAX theater**. The film it uses is ten times as big as normal movie film, so the picture is ultra-clear.

For some "light" entertainment, lay on the floor and watch laser lights dance in the sky to cool music. The **Boeing Spacearium** laser show plays on weekends and school holidays.

If all this has got you in the mood for a scientific toy or a dinosaur souvenir, check out the first-rate gift shop.

Nearby is the **Pacific Arts Center**, an art gallery for kids. If any art gallery would tickle your cultural fancy, this is it. It's free and filled with art by, for, and of the children.

Seattle Children's Museum is a child-size adult neighborhood. It's filled with super-creative hands-on exhibits and programs especially for kids from 3 to 10 years old. While I'm over twice that old and I had fun, a lot of cooler kids feel it's overrun with 4- and 5-year-olds.

You can be the doctor, the bus driver, or the grocery store owner while your mom or dad get to be the patient, the passenger, or the customer. You can put on your own show in the theater, make people-size bubbles, or use a stethoscope. Every day there are special workshops where you can do things like design a French cookie, grind peanuts into peanut butter, or learn about putting on make-up.

Imagination Station, a hands-on art studio right next to the Children's Museum is more interesting for older kids. Guest artists will teach you how to use a potter's wheel, weave on a loom, do silk screening and tie-dyeing, and much more. The small entrance fee includes supplies.

The Seattle Center's huge fountain is always dancing to its own music just outside the Center House. The **Northwest Crafts Center** and the flag pavilion are nearby. Can you find your state flag flapping in the wind?

8. The U, the Zoo, and Little Norway

The **University of Washington** has a cool campus, and you're welcome to walk around like one of those famous 12-year-old geniuses who are playing college while their friends are still playing Nintendo. In the center of campus you'll find the big brick **Red Square**. This is an awesome place for kids to roller skate or skateboard. Tired moms and dads appreciate the benches. If you stand between the three tall brick towers, look up at the sky, and spin around about three times, you get a fast and free visit to dizzyland. (Don't do this without a parent's supervision.) Check out the postcard view of Mount Rainier from Red Square. Weren't they smart to put that mountain there?

The campus is a friendly place, but don't feed or pet the students. If you're a stargazer, the **observatory** is open some nights and kids like you can look through its giant telescope. The **Burke Museum** offers a good look at Indian culture and also has a good cafe and gift shop.

Behind the humongous Husky Stadium is the water sports center and climbing rock. If it's sunny, why not drop by and rent a canoe or rowboat to explore the nearby arboretum. Be careful, the world-famous University of Washington crew may be practicing. They go fast enough to nearly slice through your boat without noticing the bump.

For a trip into a very strange land, paddle under the noisy freeway. It's dark, kind of spooky, and filled with the thunderous noise of all that speeding traffic. You can paddle to your own private deserted island. Back on dry land, wander over to the climbing rock where students test their rock wall-scaling skills.

The **Museum of History and Industry** sounds totally boring but actually offers the best time tunnel in Seattle. Check out the 1920s Boeing mail plane, "the flying boat." Peek into a 100-year-old barber shop. Back in those days kids didn't cry: dentists gave laughing gas instead of Novocain. Don't miss the early electric hairbrush and the very permanent way ladies got permanents. You can see clunky 1920s toasters and clumsy ancient vacuum cleaners. The "hands-on-history" section lets you dress radically old-fashioned. And before you leave, notice the giant elephant on the gift shop wall, with ears the size of tents.

The museum is a good place to start a quick walk through the marshy fields of the much-loved **arboretum**. You can pick up a free nature walk guide at the museum.

Take the little walk toward the Husky Stadium to the **totem pole** (talk about a family tree) on the Lake Washington ship canal. This is the big ditch that was dug to help connect this

#1

HISTORY of WATER SKIING ··▶

41

freshwater lake with salty Puget Sound. The canal is a perfect place to watch the boats. The bridge over on your left yawns open for tall boats. Are any coming?

The trail on the right leads to **Foster Island**. This is duck city and great for bird-watching. Walk down the soggy bark trail. Caution! One wrong step and you're all wet. The birds don't seem to mind the traffic noise, but on football Saturdays, when the stadium is filled with 50,000 screaming Husky fans, many ducks paddle south for the day.

For a more complete look at Seattle's 200-acre arboretum park, you'll need to drive or hike to the other end where you'll find a visitors center and plenty of trees to hug.

whoa! Pass the salt! This water is too fresh for me!!

Just a couple miles west of the university is Seattle's little Norway, **Ballard**. Norwegian immigrants found the Seattle area to be a lot like home—wet and green. They settled in Ballard as fishermen and loggers. Ballard was a separate town until 1907, when Seattle gobbled it up. It is still Seattle's little Scandinavia with monuments to Eric the Red, great Danish pastries, pewter shopping, lots of blondes, Sven and Ole jokes, and the Nordic Heritage Museum.

Ballard is not a wild and crazy place. It has a pleasant downtown section and three things that matter to you: the largest hobby store in the United States, the Nordic Heritage Museum, and the Hiram M. Chittenden Locks with their fish ladder.

*In downtown Ballard, you'll find the hobbyland of your dreams. It's a funky cluttered store called **American Eagles** which has over 90,000 toys and 20,000 miniature soldiers and mutant ninja everything. The store carries every role-playing, strategy, and lead miniatures game published in the United States.*

If you have even a drop of Scandinavian blood, Ballard's **Nordic Heritage Museum** is a good way to learn how your great-grandparents got all the way to this country. In this clever museum, you'll actually walk through the journey from the old country, on the boat—no luxury cruise ships back in those days—past the Statue of Liberty and into the depressing slums of New York. Life was so crummy for newcomers that most went west in covered wagons. Many ended up right here in Ballard. You'll see a grassy sod house, a 1,500-pound bear (stuffed) more than twice as tall as you are, old dresses, fishing gear, skis, and furniture from each Scandinavian country.

Early Seattle spent a lot of its time pushing and pulling giant logs around. With two big lakes in their city, early pioneers dreamed of cutting a path to the sea so they could float those logs

SomeHow I DoN'T think this Bear is named Teddy.

HOW LOCKS WORK

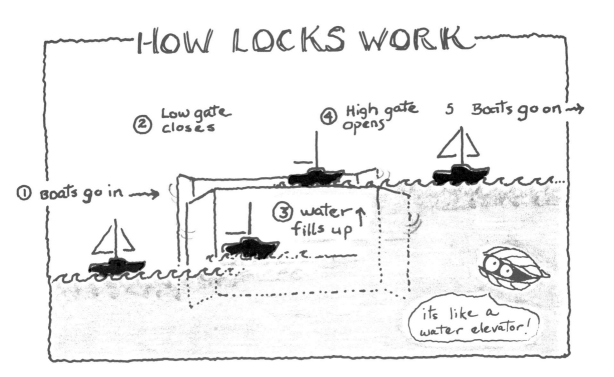

① Boats go in ⟶

② Low gate closes

③ water fills up ↑

④ High gate opens

⑤ Boats go on ⟶

its like a water elevator!

and lots of other stuff to the saltwater harbor.

Slicing holes to connect these lakes with the Puget Sound was a big job. Many miles of dirt had to be moved. The American government was in a canal-building mood. It was building the much bigger Panama Canal at the same time and decided to give the dreamers in Seattle some money to help make their dream come true. In 1917, the locks were opened. Now over 100,000 boats a year pass slowly through the **Hiram M. Chittenden Locks**.

Locks are like elevators for boats. The fresh-water lakes of Seattle are about 26 feet higher than the sea. Boats sail into the big box of water from the lake. The door closes and the water is drained out until the boats are lowered to sea level. Then the other door is opened and the

Ballard has some crazy urban sculpture. The wackiest (at the north end of the Fremont bridge) is a group of stone-faced commuters whose bus never comes. And, be careful! Hiding under the north end of the nearby giant Aurora bridge is a giant troll ready to pounce and roll.

Ask a worker about Hershel, the famous local sea lion. Hershel discovered that he had his private all-you-can-eat (up to 10,000 a day) fish bar here. "Hershel" is actually many persistent sea lions. Although they've been trucked hundreds of miles away, they keep swimming back to this place for the best free lunch on the West Coast.

boats sail away into the salt water. The locks also work to raise boats from the lower sea level to the higher lake level.

Start your visit at the visitors' center. The short slide show is interesting for the history of this giant ditch-digging project. Upstairs you can push a button and watch a model lock in action to learn how it works.

Then head out to see the real locks in action. There are two, a giant one that works only for huge boats and on very busy days and the much smaller one. Watch the water coming in and then draining out. Don't straddle the gates when they open! Walk over the long spillway that regulates the level of the lakes. Notice the 26-foot drop in water levels—fresh water on your left and the salty stuff way down there on your right.

Since no mortal fish can jump 26 feet high, and many fish need to go back to where they

A "FISH LADDER"

SALTY
PUGET
SOUND
WATER

were born to lay their eggs, a fish ladder has been built. This watery staircase for migrating fish helps them get used to the fresh water gradually.

Special windows allow you to see the hard-working pregnant fish fighting their way back to their birthplace. About 500,000 fish a year use this ladder. In the summer, salmon climb the ladder; in the winter, it's steelhead. Summer, November, and January are the best times for fish-watching. But drop by anytime to see who's in the ladder. Could you return to your birth-place without a map or mom? Each one of these fish can. They don't use a guidebook, they use instinct.

Back by the car park there's a lush garden with about 1,000 different kinds of trees, plants, and flowers from around the world. Looking for a Japanese witch hazel? You'll find it here.

Seattle's **Woodland Park Zoo** is one of the ten

Seattle Children's Theater (PONCHO Theater), in Woodland park at N. 50th St. and Fremont Ave. N., 633-4567, is one of the best of its kind with a much respected season running from September through June.

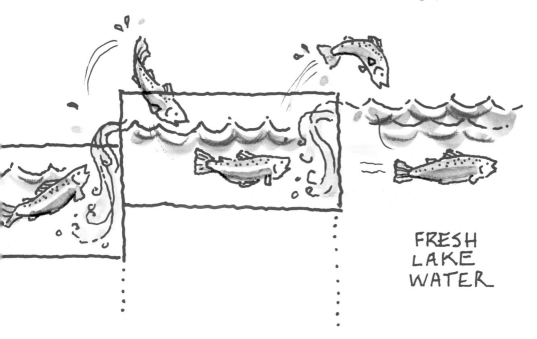

FRESH
LAKE
WATER

best in the U.S. It really knows how to make all the animals feel at home, not "in cage." Drop by to see the great new elephant house. You can shake hands with a hairy, snorty trunk! In the nocturnal house the zookeeper has switched day and night around so the animals think your daytime is a dark, muggy tropical night. Spend some time hanging around with the bats and sloths. The Savannah land transfers you to far-away Africa for a peek at the zebras and their buddies in their nearly real home. Check out those reptiles, get grossed out by gorillas picking their noses, march behind a peacock trumpeter on parade, ride a pony, and make friends with plain old, ordinary teenage turtles. More than 500 kinds of animals live here. Don't miss the family farm where human kids can meet and pet their animal counterparts. For close encounters of the furry kind, call the zoo for special family events, zookeeper talks, and tours.

Let's Eat Fish!
The **Lock Spot Cafe** at the entry to the park has a handy fast food bar outside or a family dining inside. If you worked up an appetite watching the fish climb their ladder, you can eat one of them here. Unlike Hershel, you'll have to pay for your fish.

9. Parks, Beaches, Sports, and Day Trips

Here's a quick rundown on Seattle's most popular parks and beaches. The 3-mile path around little **Green Lake** is Seattle's favorite jogging path. It's great for nature-watching and people-watching. There's a well-equipped playground with an indoor swimming pool on the northeast side. It's fun to bike, skate, or skateboard around the lake. Rent gear on the southeast side of the lake at Greg's Greenlake Cycle or Rainbow Skates and Skateboards. To rent a boat, try Green Lake Boat

Rentals (northeast side of the lake) or the Green Lake Small Craft Center (southwest corner of the lake). For a good basic burger joint, eat at Greenlake Jake's. It's famous for burgers, blueberry muffins, and breakfasts (just off the north shore). Nearby, Guido's serves tasty pizza by the slice. Twin Tepees on Aurora Avenue is another good place to eat.

Windy and grassy **Gas Works Park** on Lake Union is famous for kite flying. You can watch or, if you want your own, buy or rent a kite from the Gasworks Kite Shop. The park has great views and picnic shelters. Nearby, on Stone Way, check out "Archie McPhee's"—a warehouse of rubber snakes, X-ray specs, magic gadgets, and goofy tricks.

Volunteer Park, on top of Capitol Hill, has a

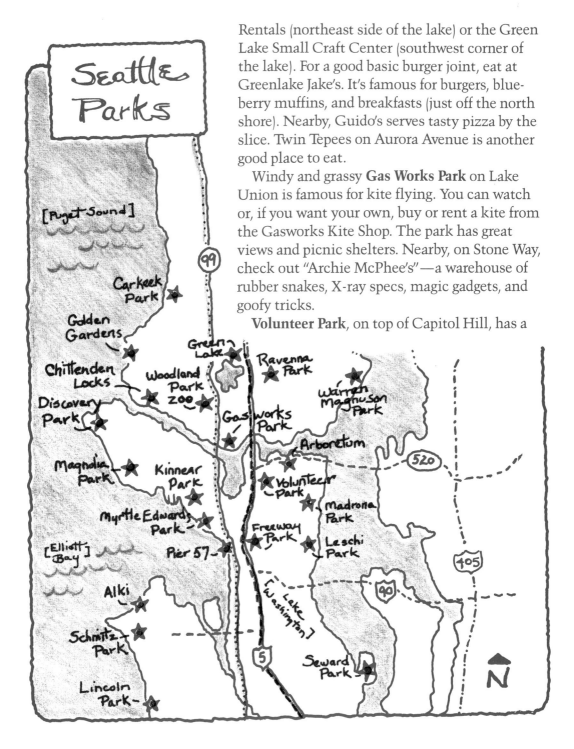

Seattle Parks

[Puget Sound]

Carkeek Park

Golden Gardens

Chittenden Locks

Discovery Park

Magnolia Park

Kinnear Park

Myrtle Edwards Park

[Elliott Bay]

Pier 57

Alki

Schmitz Park

Lincoln Park

Green Lake

Woodland Park Zoo

Gasworks Park

Ravenna Park

Warren Magnuson Park

Arboretum

Volunteer Park

Freeway Park

Madrona Park

Leschi Park

[Lake Washington]

Seward Park

N

historic cemetery, a conservatory with exotic flowers and plants, and a free, 75-foot water tower climb for a great city view.

Discovery Park, a former army base with 534 green acres and sandy seacliffs, features guided nature walks, exercise trails, plenty of marine, meadow, and stream life, and two great playgrounds. The **Daybreak Star Arts Center** keeps Indian arts and crafts alive and on sale.

Burke-Gilman Trail might be the skinniest park anywhere. It's a 24-mile-long, grassy former train track stretching from Gasworks Park on Lake Union to the Logboom Park in Kenmore at the north end of Lake Washington. Locals like it, and it's crowded on weekends. It's ideal for biking (rent a bike at the Bicycle Center) and has several waterfront restaurants along the way.

Day Trips

Seattle is surrounded by interesting and easy places to visit.

The **Museum of Flight** at Boeing Field has a six-story steel and glass Great Gallery filled with a huge indoor fleet of historic planes frozen in flight. It shows the story of flight from Leonardo da Vinci to the space shuttle. There are free movies about historic flights, the original Boeing "red barn," and free guided tours. Visit the hands-on learning area called the "Hangar." Most schoolday mornings, it's filled with flying toys—boomerangs, kites, paper airplanes, and more. The best bird's-eye view of all the planes is from the mezzanine balcony. For the real thing, you can watch test flights take off and land just beyond the parking lot on the Boeing airstrip. And check out some of the fun souvenirs: flying models, space pens that write upside down, and astronaut ice cream (it's dehydrated; your spit brings it back to life).

The **Boeing Everett Plant** (north of Seattle on

Gas Works Park is the perfect kite flyer's launch pad. At sunset, the views are great. Seattle seems to float on Lake Unicon and glow. Bring your camera and a picnic dinner. Oh, and keep an eye on Mom and Dad—this can be quite a romantic spot.

51

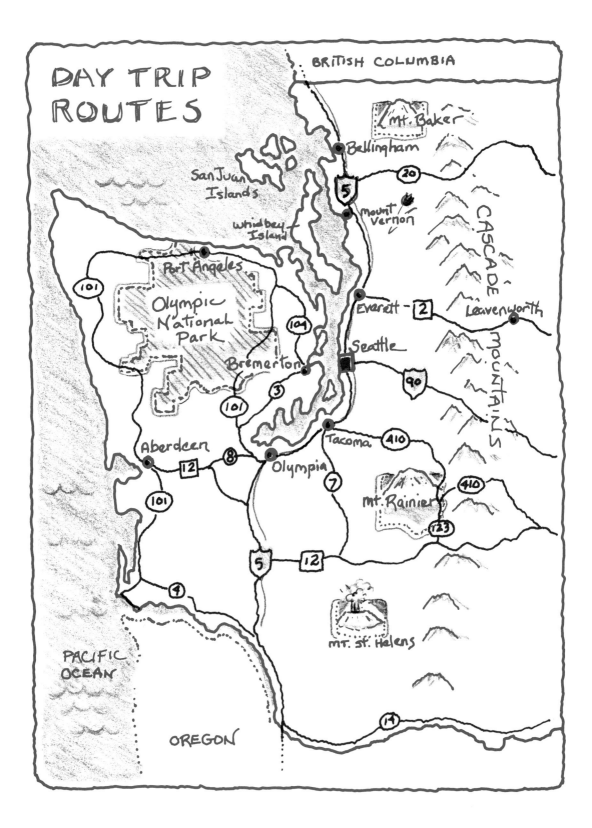

Highway 526) gives free 90-minute tours with a slide and movie presentation and a visit to the largest building in the world. Call for times. They strictly enforce their age limit: no one under 10 is admitted.

Washington is called the Evergreen State. For some hands-on nature and a sampling of the good old days, you can take a short drive out of the city to places like these: **Pioneer Farm Museum** in Eatonville, where you can become a farm kid 100 years ago, milk a cow, make a horse-shoe, jump in hay, ride a pony, and even over-night in a hay loft; **Gold Creek Trout Farm** in Woodinville; or **Breazeale-Padillo Bay Interpreta-tive Center** in Mt. Vernon, where you can see sea animals, join mud-flat safaris in the summer months, feel the fur board, look through micro-scopes, and take field trips and walks.

Or, if you just want to be wet and wild, visit **Enchanted Village**, for a giant wave pool, a river ride, an activity pool, rides, picnic areas, and a pet zoo.

Olympic National Park offers lush wilderness, rain forest hikes, great trout, steelhead, and salmon fishing, and mineral hot springs to soak in. You can drive around the Olympic Peninsula in a very long day. Don't miss the rugged ocean beaches and the **Hoh River Rain Forest**.

The Cascade mountain range is full of attrac-tions. **Mount Rainier**, that 14,400-foot-tall ice cream cone on Seattle's horizon, is also a reward-ing day trip. The famous local volcano, **Mount St. Helens**, is just south of Mount Rainier. You'll find a helpful visitor's center there.

If you drive two hours west of Seattle, you'll be in **Leavenworth**, a popular little fake German town. Seattle-ites know if you're really tired of

Seattle is the only city in the Northwest to have major league teams in all three big sports: the Sea-hawks (football in the Kingdome, tel. 827-9777), the Mariners (baseball in the Kingdome, tel. 628-3556), and the Super Sonics (basketball in the Seattle Center Coliseum, tel. 281-5800).

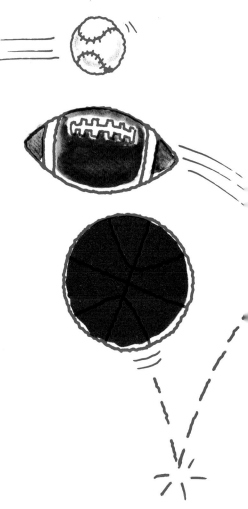

Ferry Routes

all the drizzly weather, you simply drive "east of the mountains."

A **ferry ride** from downtown across the Puget Sound to Winslow offers a fun and scenic 30-minute trip on the newest and biggest Washington ferries (leaving throughout the day from Pier 52). It's just a short walk off the ferry on Bainbridge Island into downtown Winslow. For a fun and hearty breakfast or wholesome lunch, eat at the **Streamliner Diner**. For ferry schedule information, call 464-6400.

You can ride a Washington State Ferry (464-6400) to the remote and beautiful **San Juan Islands**. Shaw Island has the world's only ferry landing run by nuns. Take a walk up Mount Constitution on the island named by a Spanish explorer for the viceroy of Mexico, Don Juan Vicente de Guemes Pacheco y Padilla Orcasitas y Aguayo, Conde de Revilla Gigedo. (You can just call it Orcas for short.) On San Juan Island, look at and listen to 16 species of whales at the **Whale Museum** in Friday Harbor. From Anacortes, there is a beautiful cruise by ferry to **Victoria**, a very English town in Canada.

10. Going Home with a Bit of Chief Seattle

It's always exciting to leave home for a faraway place. And it's just as great to get back home. But you've learned and grown since you left. I bet your souvenirs include more than a Seattle T-shirt, soggy shoes, and pet seagulls. You're taking home a better understanding of our great world. A great souvenir of your trip might be a deeper understanding of the Northwest Indian philosophy. These words, written in memory of the great Chief Seattle, might be what he would have said to the people who now live and play in the city that bears his name:

> We are part of the earth and it is part of us. The perfumed flowers are our sisters; the deer, the horse, the great eagle, these are our brothers. This shining water that moves in the streams and rivers is not just water but the blood of our ancestors.

> The white man does not understand our ways. The earth is not his brother, but his enemy. When he has conquered it, he moves on. He treats his mother, the earth, and his brother, the sky, as things to be bought, plundered, sold like sheep or bright beads.

*His appetite will devour the earth
and leave behind only a desert. If all
the beasts were gone, man would die
from a great loneliness of spirit. For
whatever happens to the beasts, soon
happens to man.*

*This we know: the earth does not
belong to man; man belongs to the
earth. Man did not weave the web of
life: he is merely a strand in it. Whatever he does to the web, he does to
himself.*

With thoughts like that, I can see why he was
a chief! Travel is neat because it teaches us about
different people and places. Travel stretches your
comfort zone. Your neighborhood gets global.
And pretty soon we see ourselves as citizens of
this whole planet!

Even a young and not-so-huge city like Seattle
is filled with fascinating history, friendly people,
and beautiful natural wonders. Amazingly
enough, just about every corner of this huge world
is as interesting and precious. There's a lot to see,
a lot to live for, and a lot to take care of.

Happy travels, always!

11. Calendar for Kids

Seattle screams and giggles with fun kids' activities. Here are a few of the major kids' events of the year. For a complete listing of events during the month you'll be in Seattle, send $1.50 to Seattle's Child, P.O. Box 22578, Seattle, WA 98122; or call 206/322-2594.

Mid-Feb-early April—Whirligig, a free or very cheap festival of rides, music, and games at the Seattle Center House, 684-7200

April-September—Seattle Mariners baseball season, 628-3555

Early April—Skagit Valley Tulip Festival, 65 miles north of Seattle in Mt. Vernon. Lots of colorful street activity, parades, and flowers. Just dial 1-42-TULIP.

Early May—For 5 days, kids' performers from around the world converge on the Seattle Center to entertain the young and old alike.

May 17—Norway's Independence Day activities in Ballard and Poulsbo (12 miles northwest of Winslow). Lots of Nordic fun music, food, and carnival activities. Even if you're not into lutefisk, it's fun to put on a Viking horn hat and eat herring. Call 1-779-4848.

Memorial Day weekend—The Northwest Folklife Festival, the nation's largest folkfest, takes place in the Seattle Center. The Pike Place Market competes with clowns and color just down the street with its own festival.

3rd weekend of July through 1st Sunday in August—Seafair, Seattle's summer blowout with hydroplane races of Lake Washington, ethnic festivals in several areas, parades, and children's events at Green Lake. Call 623-7000.

First half of September—The Puyallup Fair (35 miles south of Seattle). This is a real shin kickin' rural country fair with a rodeo, animals, rides, fun food, and lots of junk. Call 1-845-1771.

September through December—Football season. The UW Huskies play on Saturdays (543-2200), and the NFL Seahawks play on Sundays (827-9766).

November through April—Super Sonics basketball season. Call 281-5850.

December—Lots of Christmas activities including the parade of the Christmas ships, *A Christmas Carol* production (ACT theatre, 285-5110), *The Nutcracker* (Pacific Northwest Ballet, 547-5900), and the window displays of the major stores in downtown.

Seattle Youth Symphony—Call 623-2001 for a concert schedule.

Pick up the *Seattle Weekly* at a newsstand for a list of what's happening in the city and what Seattle-ites are talking about. Each Friday, the *Seattle P-I* newspaper's "What's Happening" section and the *Seattle Times* "Tempo" magazine lists current entertainment especially for kids.

Nitty Gritty Index

American Eagles Hobby Shop
2220 NW Market St.
206/782-8448

Arboretum
206/543-8800

Archie McPhee's
3510 Stone Way N.
206/547-2467

Bicycle Center
4529 Sand Point Way NE
1 mile northwest of University of Washington
206/523-8300

Boat House, Waterfront Activities Center
University of Washington
206/543-9433
Mon.-Fri. 10:00 a.m.-7:30 p.m., Sat. and Sun.
9:00 a.m.-7:30 p.m.

Boeing Everett Plant Tour
north of Seattle on Highway 526 in Everett
206/342-4801; tours at 9:00 a.m. & 1:00 p.m.
Monday-Friday, no one under 10 years old

Boeing Spacearium
Pacific Science Center in Seattle Center
206/443-2850

Breazeale-Padillo Bay Interpretative Center
Mt. Vernon
206/428-1558
Wed.-Sun. 10:00 a.m.-5:00 p.m.

Burke Museum
17th Ave. NE and NE 45th St.
on UW campus
206/543-5590

Childrens' Museum
Center House, Seattle Center
206/441-1768
Tues.-Sun. 10:00 a.m.-5:00 p.m.

Coast Guard Traffic Center
Pier 36
206/286-5640

Daybreak Star Arts Center
Discovery Park
206/285-4425

Discovery Park
3801 W. Government Way
206/386-4236

El Puerco Lloron Mexican restaurant
Pike Place Market Hillclimb, 1501 Western Ave.
206/624-0541

Elliott Bay Bookshop
101 S. Main (1st and Main)
206/624-6600

Emmett Watson's Oyster Bar
1916 Pike Place
206/448-7721

Enchanted Village
36201 Enchanted Parkway South
Federal Way
206/838-8828
11:00 a.m.-8:00 p.m. daily

Freeway Park
6th Ave. and Seneca, downtown

Fun Forest Amusement Park
Seattle Center
206/728-1585
closed in winter

Funplex, Seattle
1541 15th W, 1 mile north of the piers
206/285-7842

Gasworks Kite Shop
3333 Wallingford Ave. N.
206/633-4780

Glass House Art Glass
311 Occidental Ave. S.
206/682-9939
10:00 a.m.-5:00 p.m., demos until about 3:00 p.m.

Gold Creek Trout Farm
Woodinville, 15844 148th NE
206/483-1415

Greenlake Boat Rentals
7351 E. Green Lake Dr. N.
206/527-0171

Greenlake Jakes
7918 E. Green Lake Dr. N.
206/523-4747

Greg's Greenlake Cycle
7007 Woodlawn NE
206/523-1822

Guido's
7902 E. Green Lake Dr. N.
206/522-5553

Hiram M. Chittenden Locks and Visitors' Center
3015 NW 54th St.
206/783-7059
10:00 a.m.-7:00 p.m. daily in summer, 11:00
a.m.-5:00 p.m. Thurs.-Mon. during school year

House of Hong
409 8th South, corner of 8th and Jackson
206/622-7997

IMAX Theater
Pacific Science Theater
206/443-4629

Iron Horse Restaurant
311 3rd Ave. S.
206/223-9506

Ivar's Acres of Clams and Fish Bar
Pier 54
206/624-6852

King Cafe
723 S. King St.
206/622-6373

Kingdome Tours
201 S. King St.
206/296-3128
daily, unless there's an event at 11:00 a.m., 1:00
p.m., 3:00 p.m.; Mon.-Sat. mid-April through
mid-Sept.

Klondike Gold Rush Museum
117 S. Main
206/442-7220
daily 9:00 a.m.-5:00 p.m.; 30-minute, free walking tours of Pioneer Square on summer
afternoons

Magic Mouse
1st and Yesler
206/682-8097

Monorail
Seattle Center to Westlake Center
206/684-7200
9:00 a.m.-9:00 p.m. Sun.-Thurs.,
9:00 a.m.-midnight Fri. and Sat.

Museum of Flight
9404 E. Marginal Way S.
206/764-5720
open daily 10:00 a.m.-5:00 p.m., until 9:00 p.m.
on Thurs.
exit #158 off freeway between downtown and the
airport, follow signs north on E. Marginal Way to
glass building on right.

Museum of History and Industry
2700 24th Ave E.
206/324-1125
daily 10:00 a.m.-5:00 p.m.

Nordic Heritage Museum
3014 NW 67th St.
206/789-5707
Tues.-Sat. 10:00 a.m.-4:00 p.m., Sun. 12:00-4:00 p.m.

Observatory
University of Washington
206/543-0126

Ocean City Restaurant
609 S. Weller, near Uwajimaya
206/623-2333

Old Spaghetti Factory
2801 Elliott and Broad, across from Pier 70
206/441-7724
daily 5:00 p.m.-10:00 p.m.
No reservations, usually a 30-min. wait, get name
on list and explore Pier 70.

Omnidome Theater
Pier 59
206/622-1868
Daily 10:00 a.m.-6:00 p.m. or later, showing every
half hour. Special combo ticket to theater and
aquarium is discounted.

Pacific Arts Center
Seattle Center
206/443-5437
Mon.-Sat. 10:00 a.m.-5:00 p.m., closed Sun.

Pacific Science Center
In Seattle Center
206/443-2001
Mon.-Fri. 10:00 a.m.-5:00 p.m.; Sat., Sun., holidays until 6:00 p.m.; July through September
until 6:00 p.m. daily

Peerless Pie
1930 Pike Place
206/443-1801

Pier 70 Restaurant and Chowder House
Foot of Alaska Way and Broad St.
206/728-7071

Pike Place Market General Information
206/682-7453

Pioneer Farm Museum
Eatonville, 7716 Ohop Valley Road
206/832-6300

Poncho Childrens' Theater
N. 50th St. and Fremont Ave N. at Woodlawn
Park
206/633-4567

Ruby Montana's
2nd and James
206/621-7669

Seattle Aquarium
Pier 59
206/386-4300, 386-4320 for recorded info.
10:00 a.m.-5:00 p.m. daily, until 7:00 p.m. from
Memorial Day to Labor Day.

Seattle Center
General info. 206/684-7200

Seattle Library
4th and Madison
206/386-4636
Mon.-Thurs. 9:00 a.m.-9:00 p.m., until 6:00 p.m.
on weekends

Smith Tower
506 2nd Ave. (2nd and Yesler)
next to Rick's Tower Grill
206/682-9393
Buy elevator ticket at the G and G cigar shop next
to the elevator and ask for a history sheet. Wait at
elevator #8 for the express ride to the top.

Space Needle
Seattle Center
206/443-2100

Streamliner Diner
397 Winslow Way, Winslow
206/842-8595

Tillicum Village Harbor Cruise and Dinner
Pier 56
206/329-5700
4-hour cruises almost daily; early trips for free
time on island in summer

Twin Tepees
7201 Aurora N., near Greenlake
206/783-9740

Underground Seattle Tour
Doc Maynard's Restaurant
(on the square at 610 1st Ave.)
206/682-4646 for reservations, 682-1511 for
recorded info.

Uwajimaya
519 6th Ave. S.
206/624-6248

Volunteer Park
At 15th and Galen St.,
top of Capitol Hill

Washington State Ferries
Pier 52
206/464-6400
Daily service across the Puget Sound

Westlake Center
1601 5th Ave.
206/467-1600

Wing Luke Asian Museum
407 7th Ave. S.
206/623-5124
Tues.-Fri. 11:00 a.m.-4:30 p.m.,
Sat. and Sun. 12:00-4:00 p.m.

Wood Shop
320 1st Ave. S.
206/624-1763

Woodland Park Zoo
5500 Phinney Ave. N.
206/684-4800
Daily 10:00 a.m.-5:00 p.m., sometimes later

Ye Olde Curiosity Shoppe
Pier 54
206/682-5844
9:30 a.m.-6:00 p.m., until 9:00 p.m. Fri. and Sat.

**Want to be a travel writer and researcher?
I'd love your help. If you send me your tips,
gripes, and favorite discoveries, I'll share
them with lots of other travelers in the
next edition of *Kidding Around Seattle*.
Write to me, Rick Steves, at 109 4th Ave.
N, Box C-2009, Edmonds, WA 98020.
Thanks.**

Kidding Around with John Muir Publications

We are making the world more accessible for young travelers. In your hand you have one of several John Muir Publications guides written and designed especially for kids. We will be *Kidding Around* other cities also. Send us your thoughts, corrections, and suggestions. We also publish other nonfiction young readers titles as well as adult books about travel and other subjects. Let us know if you would like one of our catalogs. All the titles below are 64 pages and $9.95, except for *Kidding Around the National Parks of the Southwest* and *Kidding Around Spain*, which are 108 pages and $12.95 each.

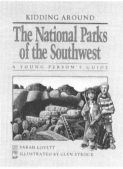

TITLES NOW
AVAILABLE IN THE
SERIES
Kidding Around Atlanta
Kidding Around Boston
Kidding Around Chicago
Kidding Around the Hawaiian Islands
Kidding Around London
Kidding Around Los Angeles
Kidding Around the National Parks of the Southwest
Kidding Around New York City
Kidding Around Paris
Kidding Around Philadelphia
Kidding Around San Diego
Kidding Around San Francisco
Kidding Around Santa Fe
Kidding Around Seattle
Kidding Around Spain
Kidding Around Washington, D.C.

Ordering Information
Your books will be sent to you via UPS (for U.S. destinations). UPS will not deliver to a P.O. Box; please give us a street address. Include $3.75 for the first item ordered and $.50 for each additional item to cover shipping and handling costs. For airmail within the U.S., enclose $4.00. All foreign orders will be shipped surface rate; please enclose $3.00 for the first item and $1.00 for each additional item. Please inquire about foreign airmail rates.

Method of Payment
Your order may be paid by check, money order, or credit card. We cannot be responsible for cash sent through the mail. All payments must be made in U.S. dollars drawn on a U.S. bank. Canadian postal money orders in U.S. dollars are acceptable. For VISA, MasterCard, or American Express orders, include your card number, expiration date, and your signature, or call (800) 888-7504. Books ordered on American Express cards can be shipped only to the billing address of the cardholder. Sorry, no C.O.D.'s. Residents of sunny New Mexico, add 5.875% tax to the total.

Address all orders and inquiries to:
John Muir Publications
P.O. Box 613
Santa Fe, NM 87504
(505) 982-4078
(800) 888-7504